ANIMALS ARE AMAZING

WOLVES

BY KATE RIGGS

W
FRANKLIN WATTS
LONDON•SYDNEY

Franklin Watts
First published in Great Britain in 2015 by
The Watts Publishing Group

Credits
Series Designer: The Design Lab
Art Direction: Rita Marshall
Picture Credits: Photographs by Dreamstime (Pwozza,
Skynesher, Stephenmeese), Getty Images (Georgette
Douwma, Mustafa Ozer/AFP, Flip Nicklin, Gail
Shumway, Stuart Westmorland, Norbert Wu), and iS-
tockphoto (Lars Christensen, Jose Manuel Gelpi Diaz,
Nancy Nehring, Tammy Peluso, James Steidl)

Every attempt has been made to clear copyright.
Should there be any inadvertent omission please
apply to the publisher for rectification.

Dewey number: 599.773
HB ISBN: 978 1 4451 4517 4

Printed in China

MIX
Paper from
responsible sources
FSC® C104740
www.fsc.org

Franklin Watts
An imprint of
Hachette Children's Group
Part of The Watts Publishing Group
Carmelite House
50 Victoria Embankment
London EC4Y 0DZ

An Hachette UK Company
www.hachette.co.uk

www.franklinwatts.co.uk

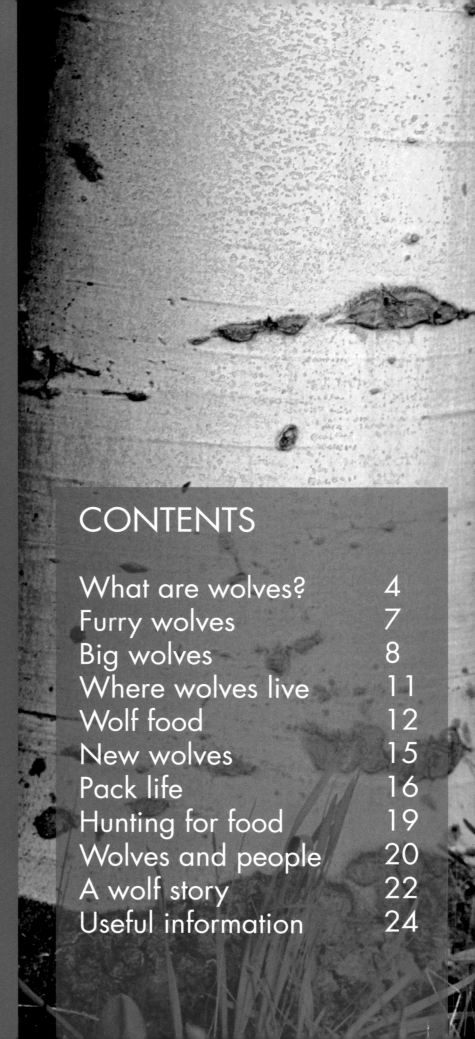

CONTENTS

What are wolves?

Grey wolves are also called 'timber wolves'.

Wolves are big, wild dogs. There are many **species** of wolf, such as the red wolf and the grey wolf. There are many kinds of grey wolf, including the **Arctic** wolf and the Mexican wolf.

species different types of an animal that all share the same name.
Arctic the very cold area around the North Pole, which is often covered with snow and ice.

Furry wolves

Grey wolves have thick fur and a bushy tail. Although they are called grey wolves, their fur can be grey, white, black, red or brown. Red wolves have shorter fur than grey wolves. They look like big foxes.

Red wolves have bigger ears than most other wolves. They can hear very well.

Big wolves

Male grey wolves are the biggest wolves. They normally weigh around 45 kilogrammes but can weigh up to 80 kilogrammes! Males are about 1.5 metres long. Female wolves are a little smaller than male wolves.

Grey wolves are much bigger than most types of pet dog.

Where wolves live

Most grey wolves live in the Northern **Hemisphere**. Many of these places are very cold and snowy. Some grey wolves live near mountains, others live in forests. Red wolves live in the southeastern part of the United States.

Many grey wolves are happy to live in a very cold **habitat**.

hemisphere one of the two halves of the Earth on either side of the Equator. One half is called the Northern Hemisphere, the other half is called the Southern Hemisphere.
habitat the natural home of an animal or plant.

Wolf food

Wolves are carnivores, which means they eat meat. They can eat up to 10 kilogrammes of food in one meal. Some of their favourite animals to eat are moose and deer. Wolves also eat smaller animals, such as rabbits, birds and fish.

These wolves have caught and will eat this deer.

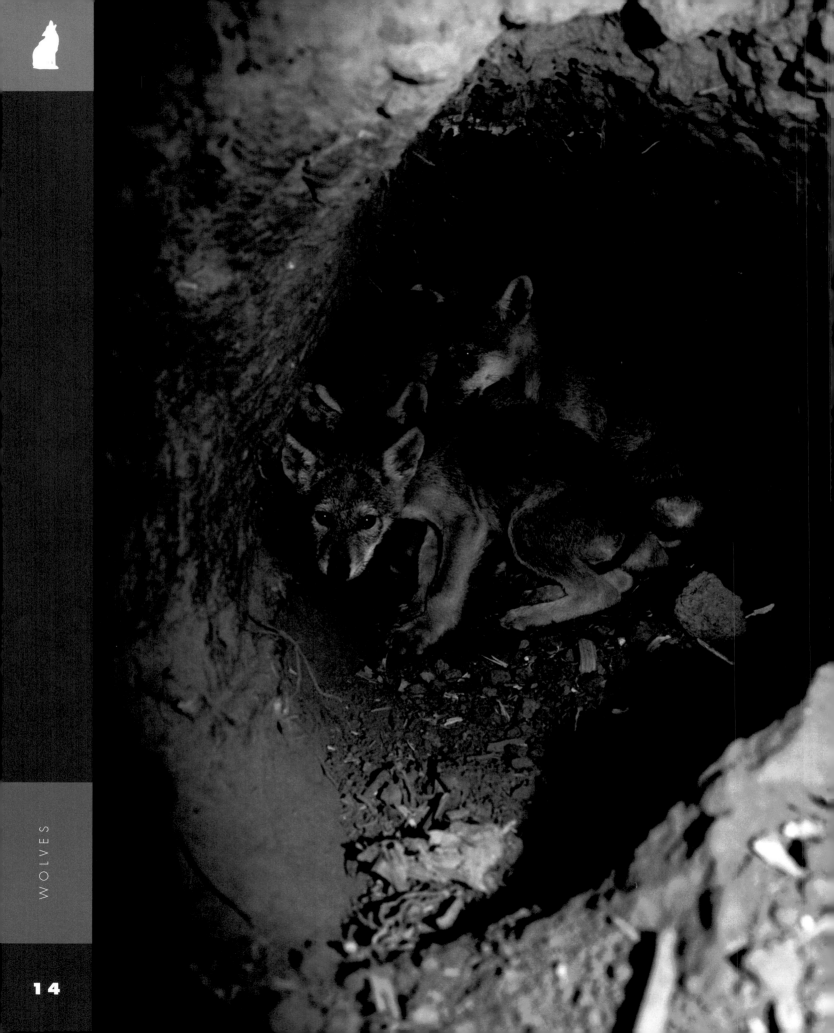

New wolves

A female wolf has between four and seven **pups** at a time. At first, the pups live in a **den** to stay safe. When the pups are about two months old, they leave the den and start learning how to hunt. Wild wolves can live for up to twelve years.

Wolf pups hide in their den when their mother is out hunting.

pups baby wolves.
den a home that is hidden, like a cave.

Pack life

Wolves live in groups called packs. Most packs have between six and eleven wolves. Two wolves called the alpha (*Al-fah*) male and the alpha female lead the pack. Wolves spend a lot of time sleeping, hunting and moving around their **territory**.

Wolves have very good eyesight and can see well in the dark.

territory the area that a pack of wolves lives in. Each pack has its own territory.

Hunting for food

Wolves are **predators** and they spend a lot of time looking for food. They hunt for up to ten hours every day. The pack works together to chase **prey**. Wolves have to run fast to catch a deer or a moose!

Grey wolves can run at 60 kilometres per hour – that's as fast as a car!

predators animals that eat other animals.
prey animals that are eaten by other animals.

Wolves and people

In the past there were lots of wolves in the wild. People hunted wolves to stop them killing farm animals. Today there are fewer wolves, but the numbers of wolves in the wild are growing. Some people go to see wolves at zoos or in the wild. It is exciting to see these beautiful animals and hear them howl!

Wolves howl to let wolves in other packs know where they are.

A wolf story

How are wolves and dogs different? A famous man named Aesop (*EE-sop*), from ancient Greece, used to tell a story about this. One day, a hungry wolf and a well-fed dog met on a road. The dog told the wolf that he should live with people. Then he would have an easy life and a full belly because he would not have to hunt for food. Then the wolf saw the dog's collar around his neck. He realised that if he lived with people, he would not be free.

Useful information

Read More

Animal Families: Wolves by Tim Harris (Wayland, 2014)

Amazing Animals: Wolves by Jen Green (Franklin Watts, 2011)

Websites

www.wolf.org/learn/wild-kids/
The International Wolf Centre has a fantastic section on its website dedicated to kids. Learn some 'wolfy words', loads of facts and stats and have fun with the activity pages, including a 'WolfQuest' game.

www.animalfactguide.com/animal-facts/gray-wolf/
This site has a factfile on the grey wolf and links to several other wolf-related websites.

www.californiawolfcenter.org/learn/kids-activities/
This site has lots of facts and a kids' area with wolf crafts, activities and a colouring page.

Every effort has been made by the Publishers to ensure that these websites are suitable for children, that they are of the highest educational value and that they contain no inappropriate or offensive material. However, because of the nature of the Internet, it is impossible to guarantee that the contents of these sites will not be altered. We strongly advise that Internet access is supervised by a responsible adult.

Index